IT'S TIME TO EAT AN INDIAN PRUNE

It's Time to Eat an Indian Prune

Walter the Educator

Silent King Books
A WhichHead Entertainment Imprint

Copyright © 2024 by Walter the Educator

All rights reserved. No part of this book may be reproduced in any manner whatsoever without written per- mission except in the case of brief quotations embodied in critical articles and reviews.

First Printing, 2024

Disclaimer

This book is a literary work; the story is not about specific persons, locations, situations, and/or circumstances unless mentioned in a historical context. Any resemblance to real persons, locations, situations, and/or circumstances is coincidental. This book is for entertainment and informational purposes only. The author and publisher offer this information without warranties expressed or implied. No matter the grounds, neither the author nor the publisher will be accountable for any losses, injuries, or other damages caused by the reader's use of this book. The use of this book acknowledges an understanding and acceptance of this disclaimer.

It's Time to Eat an Indian Prune is a collectible early learning book by Walter the Educator suitable for all ages belonging to Walter the Educator's Time to Eat Book Series. Collect more books at WaltertheEducator.com

USE THE EXTRA SPACE TO TAKE NOTES AND DOCUMENT YOUR MEMORIES

INDIAN PRUNE

It's time for a snack, what should we choose?

It's Time to Eat an Indian Prune

How about a fruit with purple hues?

Round and plump, it's shiny and bright,

An Indian Prune, what a tasty delight!

Look at it sparkle, deep and sweet,

Perfect and ready for us to eat.

Pick one up, give it a try,

Indian Prune, oh my, oh my!

Peel it or bite right through the skin,

A juicy surprise is waiting within.

Soft and smooth, so sweet to the core,

One little bite, and you'll want more!

A bit like a plum, but all its own,

The Indian Prune has a taste that's grown.

Not too tart, not too sweet,

Just the right snack to make your day complete!

It's Time to Eat an
Indian Prune

Crunch, munch, take a nibble,

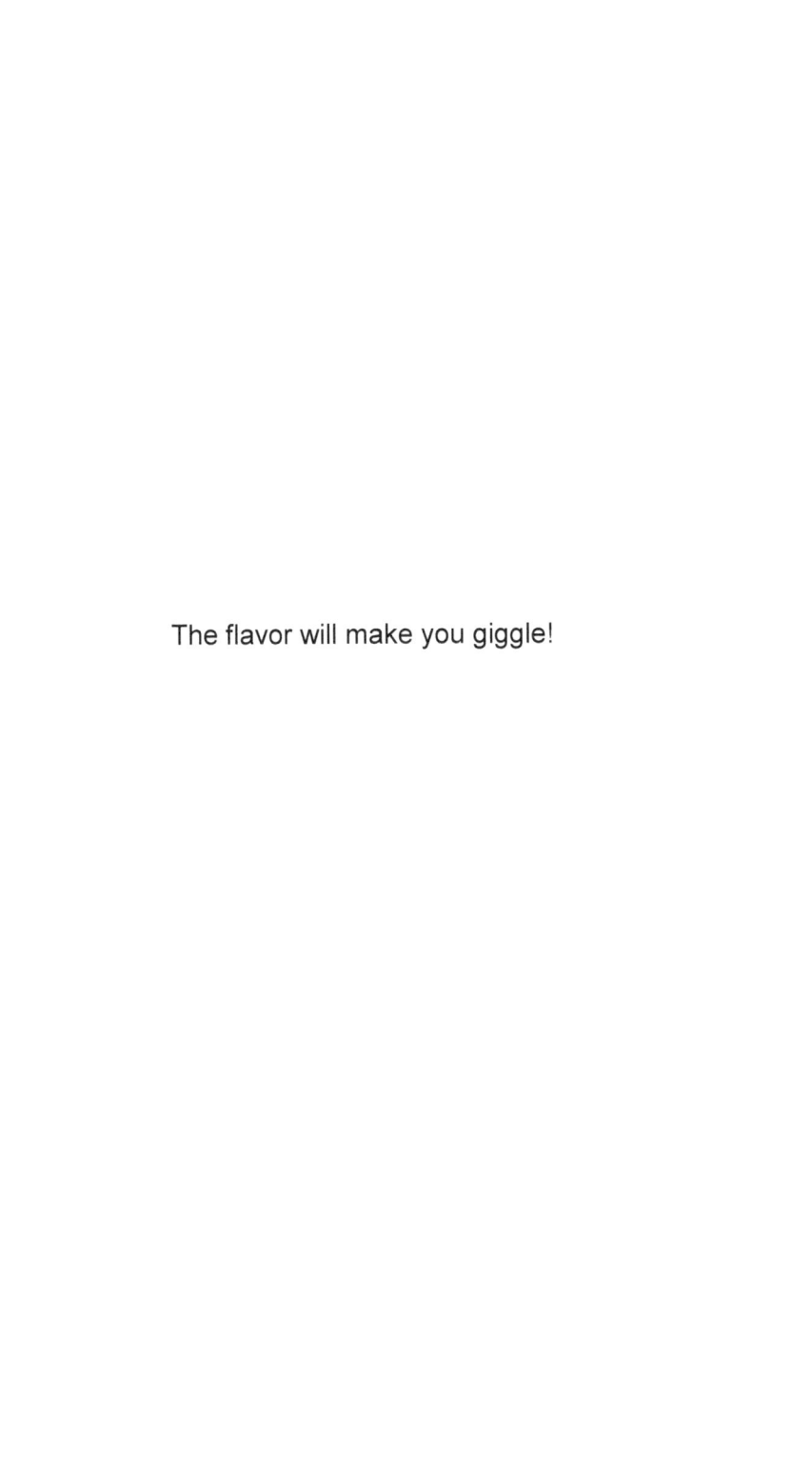

Chewy goodness in every bite,

Eating this prune feels so right!

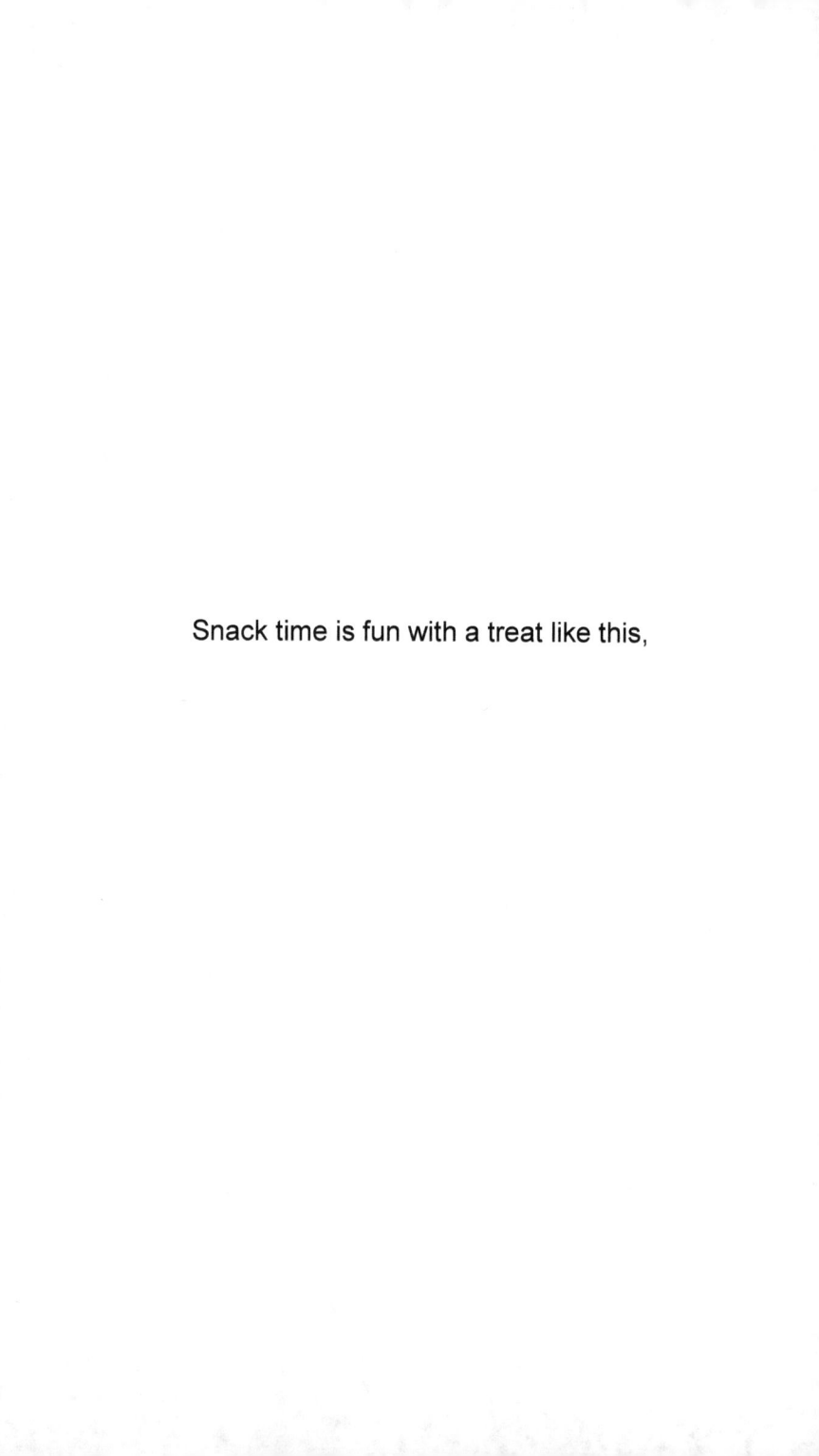

Snack time is fun with a treat like this,

Indian Prune is pure fruit bliss.

Healthy and yummy, it helps you grow,

A tasty snack that helps you glow!

Eat it plain, or mix it up,

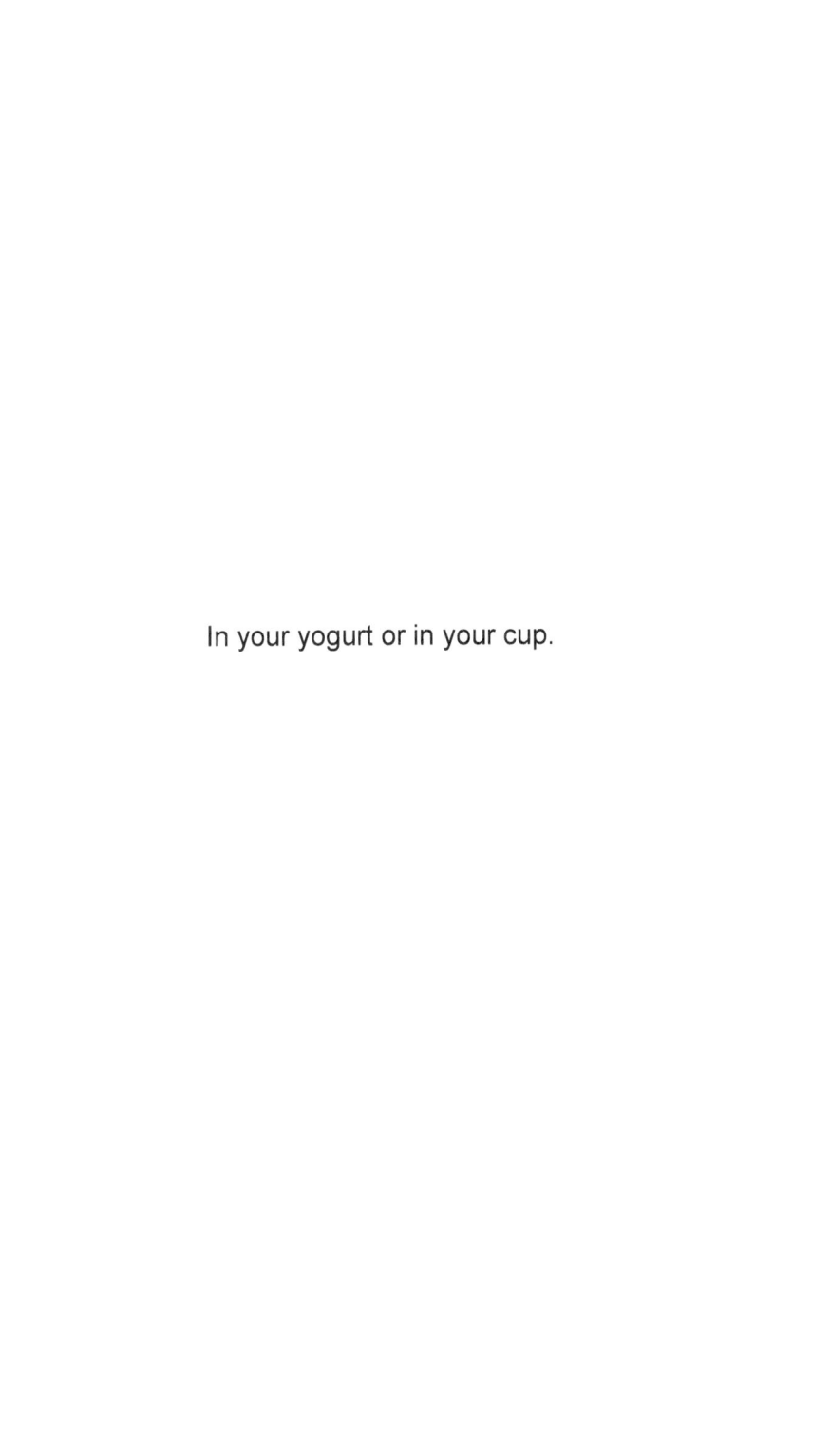

In your yogurt or in your cup.

No matter how you choose to munch,

Indian Prune is perfect for lunch!

Share with friends, don't eat alone,

This tasty treat is well-known.

Purple and soft, it's good for you,

Indian Prune will make you feel brand new!

So when it's snack time, you know what to do,

Pick an Indian Prune, that's the clue!

It's juicy, sweet, and oh so fine,

A perfect fruit for snack time shine!
It's Time to Eat an
Indian Prune

Yum, yum, yum, take a bite,

Indian Prune is pure delight!

So when you're hungry and need a treat,

An Indian Prune is fun to eat!

ABOUT THE CREATOR

Walter the Educator is one of the pseudonyms for Walter Anderson. Formally educated in Chemistry, Business, and Education, he is an educator, an author, a diverse entrepreneur, and he is the son of a disabled war veteran. "Walter the Educator" shares his time between educating and creating. He holds interests and owns several creative projects that entertain, enlighten, enhance, and educate, hoping to inspire and motivate you. Follow, find new works, and stay up to date with Walter the Educator™ at WaltertheEducator.com

www.ingramcontent.com/pod-product-compliance
Lightning Source LLC
LaVergne TN
LVHW010437070526
838199LV00066B/6061